I0075096

ENTREPRENEURSHIP

CHANGED THE WAY I

THINK

Sunny Deshpande

FIRST EDITION: Edited by Denise Joyce

ISBN: 0692189521
ISBN-13: 978-0692189528

DEDICATION

This book is dedicated to Jerry

Also by Sunny Deshpande

fineartsofsunny.com: No house is home without art. Get an experience, not just a painting.

CONTENTS

ACKNOWLEDGMENTS

I want to take time to acknowledge all the people that have helped me take this dream of writing a book and make it a reality. I want to give a big thanks to my wonderful editor, Denise Joyce, for seeing my passion with this book even when it was still in its rough draft. She worked relentlessly to perfectly put my passion into words and share my ideas with everybody around in the best way possible. I also want to sincerely acknowledge the reason of being for this book. My true friend, Jerry, pushed me to write this book and inspired the passion and drive in myself to carry out the project of writing this book. Before I met Jerry, I had never really had a friend that believed in me as much as he did. And of course, my parents helped me tremendously. Particularly, my mom, was a big help in cleaning out the very rough, initial draft of this book. Lastly, I want to thank everyone else who has also believed in me and given me confidence in striving to make the most out of my potential.

A Letter from my first customer, now one of my best friends

My name is Jerry Carlisle. My career relationship with Sunny Deshpande began after he was commissioned to render an oil painting from a photograph of my countryside home in the mountains. I later learned this was his first paid commission. I was surprisingly blown away with the end results and now own two commissions displayed in my home.

At age fifteen Sunny has mastered the art of presentation and salesmanship. My second commission was hand delivered wrapped in white linen. He selectively monogramed several personalized cards; including discussions about his artistry, goals, creative passions. I was mesmerized with his attention to details. In fact his preparation and presentation only enhanced my first glimpse of the hidden treasure beneath the layers of red ribbons, monogramed stitching he stitched after borrowing his neighbors sewing machine.

Today, we still have weekly conversations discussing his dreams and aspirations. He is an active reader and quick learner adopting sales and marketing strategies, innovation, technology and of course our passion for exotic cars and watches. Several months ago I advised Sunny to start documenting his ideas for preservation; little did I know he would achieve the unthinkable and publish his first book!

Regards,

Jerry L Carlisle

AUTHOR PREFACE

Introduction

First and foremost, this book wouldn't have been written without the encouragement of my best friend, Jerry. I would like to dedicate this book to him. A few people had been telling me to write a book, but Jerry was the one who kept pushing the idea.

I finally sat down one day and decided to make it happen. I created a vision, and just started typing until the vision became a reality. The ideas kept flowing and I kept putting them into words.

Everything I learned in the last few years has been put into this book with the goal of inspiring a wide range of ages, not just kids. I have been on an incredible journey, all the way from getting my very first art commission to transforming myself into an author, entrepreneur, and businessman.

It wasn't too long ago that I first started to think about having a business. So a few years ago, I couldn't have imagined describing myself with those titles.

I strongly believe in every one of the things I have written about here. My goal by writing this book is genuine, and I hope I will benefit many who read it.

I have learned so much through my actions. By no means am I completely accomplished or anything like that, but I will say that I have changed for the better by starting my own business as a kid. This book is meant to provide insight on exactly how entrepreneurship has brought so much into my life. People of all ages and walks of life might find thoughts and ideas here that will change their mindset toward a new and much more positive direction. I know changing my mindset changed myself.

You don't even need to be in business to learn something from this book. It's meant to inspire everyone to take those first steps toward winning more at life!

For all the kids wanting to make it big someday

Starting your own business as a kid can change your life. The whole reason I am writing this book is because of the huge benefits I have seen after having the passion and will to start my own small business. I am also a kid, so I can relate to kids who are interested in and very passionate about entrepreneurship.

The great thing about starting a business is that it not only helps you make money as a kid, but it also makes you look amazing: After all, you are running a business at such a young age!

And there's this: College admission staff look for students with good extracurricular activities, assessing how a student stands out from his peers. The reality is that everybody these days does sports, may play an instrument or two, and may be part of some club. But how many kids have started a business? Having your own small business will make you look ten times smarter than you might actually be!

The ability to make money at a young age, or at least try to, will say a lot of good things about you. Real-world experience along with a load of knowledge is always great. Running your own business will teach you skills and life-lessons you might never learn in school.

<u>Chapter one</u>

DECISIONS BROUGHT YOU HERE

Decisions set your life's course

Many people who have seen my art say that I am talented, insisting that I must have been born with a gift. But I always responded that I am just like everybody else.

Frankly, I used to say this just to be humble, but now I realize it's the truth! One day I just started wondering: What has brought me to where I am right now? I kept thinking about this, jumping from one "why" to the next. I didn't see how the answer could be that I was born more talented than somebody else, or that I just worked really hard. I thought that there had to be a deeper, but simple reason.

I finally came to one conclusion. We are born with the freedom to create our lives how we want them to be. Each and every day, our decisions shape our brains. The unique thing about us is that although it may not seem achievable, we can stretch our brains almost to infinity. There are plenty of extraordinary people out in the world, but they all have the same brain as everyone else. So, what does it all come down to at the end? Decisions.

The reason I am great at art now and have gotten attention for my abilities is because of the decisions I have made. I don't believe it was an inherited gift. When I was younger, if I had a pencil in my hand I would always create something. When I went to a restaurant and there were one of those giant papers that cover the table, I would always start creating art. My art skills kept consistently improving, leading me to acquire new skills.

At a really young age, I came across artists such as Monet and Van Gogh. In preschool and first grade, I decided to explore art and all the old masters. Even though I couldn't read back then, I looked at pictures. I was inspired by these artists, amazed at what they could create. Even in my wildest dreams I couldn't imagine being able to create art that people would want to look at, let alone pay me to create.

And then, one day I made the decision to ask my parents to take me to the Art Institute of Chicago. It was a decision that pushed my interest to new levels, and brought me to where I am: doing consistent commissions for a number of clients.

The entrepreneurship aspect of my life as a kid is linked to the first time I went door to door selling candles. It was yet another decision that ignited a new beginning.

My message is that you shape your own path. This is the reason comparing yourself to others is not beneficial. What is the point in making yourself feel bad, thinking that you are not as smart as someone else?

Healthy people all have the same potential in terms of intelligence. So, when a person says that someone is smarter than you, they are saying that that person has a better brain than you. This is not true at all! All that other person did was work harder and made the right decisions.

Remember: Every decision you make gets you to where you are today. The more you understand this, the better off you will be in knowing to make the right decisions in life.

Understanding others better by understanding the concept of decisions

Influencing other people is a big way to win at life. It can lead to enormous advantages and long-term rewards. Utilizing your social skills to do this can be challenging, and takes a much deeper understanding of how those skills work.

You need to be aware of how someone is thinking in the moment, perhaps asking yourself what sort of mood they are in.

You also need to be aware of what circumstances and decisions have brought that person to their current state of mind. This is what people with hot tempers or those who get angry easily fail to stop and think about. If you want to help someone who is having a hard time, try talking to them about what may have brought them to the point where they are now.

If you can determine what led to the current situation, you will be better equipped to address whatever issue the person is having, and you will have successfully related to that person. Really work to figure out their train of thought. It is a skill that's very important in business.

Why this emphasis on decision-making? Because it is in everything! For instance, if you are a kid and want to start a business and your parents have issues with that, think about how you can use your social skills to bring them around in their thinking. Decide to sell them on whatever it is you want to do!

Chapter two

THE SCIENCE OF RISING ABOVE PEOPLE

Take the very best people, add them to the lowest performing ones, and divide them by two. There you have your average.

Rising above this level means going beyond the plain average and into the highest performing group. But I say you should aim to be the best. Change your mindset and you can change your results. Just keep pushing.

Why great achievers move the world around them

Why do humans continue to dominate life on Earth? It's because the high achievers keep raising the bar. When you push people's notion of what defines the "best," you raise their expectations. As a result, you raise society's expectations.

If you want to move the world forward, this is the way. As you get better, the world gets better behind you. But it also will catch up to you, so you must keep pushing ahead to maintain your lead. If you become greater than great, you will inspire greatness in others.

Changing your mindset to change results

Do you ever wonder why people who become multi-millionaires and billionaires don't usually retire? Why doesn't Mark Zuckerberg drop out and just live a life of luxury on some beautiful island relaxing and taking it easy?

It's because of mindset. Robert Herjavec, from television's "Shark Tank" and founder of the Herjavec group, sold his technology company BRAK Systems and then retired. But after only a few years of retiring, it didn't feel right; he told Fortune magazine that he missed running his own company.

The "not right" feeling is actually a sense of guilt associated with going against the values of your mindset. Changing your mindset is the absolute No. 1 change you have to make to be able to manage all the steps in getting what you want.

For instance: Getting up early in the morning starts with a change in your mindset. People who say a change in results starts with a change in routine are absolutely right. But how do you change your routine and your mindset? What worked for me was creating a schedule with a detailed to-do list to motivate myself.

Imagine a child brought up by parents who are opposed to the idea of taking risks and hate rich people. They have instilled a certain way of thinking in that kid. Unfortunately, there are many people whose mindsets are focused in the wrong direction and then become locked there which lead to problems.

On the other hand, think of kids who have dreams of a better life. They are predisposed to hard work and positivity. If they are around people encouraging and embracing the values that are needed to get ahead, their mindsets will reflect this attitude.

You can even think of your mindset like your mood, which affects whether you want to do certain things. Liking something or being happy can help you get that thing done easily. Conversely, being frustrated and angry will make the same exact thing frankly seem like an impossible task.

So the first hurdle you need to clear in order to change your life toward a positive direction is changing your mindset.

Stay committed, get your vision straight

Someone once showed me how you can ignite some objects if you focus the sun's rays through a magnifying glass at them. There is abundant sunlight out there, but you can create enormous amounts of energy if you focus that sunlight into one small point than burns hotter than all of its surroundings.

The same thing happens with a telescope. The night sky appears to have little to no light. In reality, there is abundant light distributed throughout the night sky. To see the stars and the moon, you just need to gather up all the light through the telescope and use it to see the stars and the moon.

Like the magnifying glass and the telescope, you will need to focus to make an impact. Even though energy is abundant, we humans use a limited amount of it each day. Plus: If you pour energy into one thing consistently, you will grow that one thing faster than scattering a little energy into a hundred different things -- many of them useless -- each day.

If you are not focusing your energy into one thing, you are also shortening your vision! And if you are shortening your vision, you are shortening your results. You will have to push hard to get the results you are looking for. Do as much as you can, but budget your energy. Don't waste it.

I used to think it would be better if I had multiple businesses. It felt good knowing that I could tell people I was running several businesses. However, I kept telling myself that I would manage them all, but the reality was that I lost focus and my main business got off track. It just wasn't getting enough of my attention and dedication.

When I made the decision to stop the other

little ventures and just focus on my already successful business, I knew I could make it even *better*! If you truly want to succeed badly, put everything you have into one mission, and make that mission catch fire!

Get your time right

In talking about life and time, basketball great LeBron James said, "I treated it like every day was my last day with a basketball."

Time never comes back, so use it wisely and don't kid yourself that you'll live forever. Get up at 5 or 6 a.m. only because it's what you want to do for yourself. Embrace the reality of your schedule if you're busy with sports and work. Make the most out of it.

When people have a limited amount of free time, they tend to use it more wisely. But when there is an influx of time, such as during school breaks and holidays, time loses its value and boredom can set in. Be aware that you have been given the gift of life, and with that comes the responsibility of using your time wisely to do good things and live a good life. I, personally, feel that it is my responsibility to max out my potential. I know that somewhere on the other side of the world, there are people starving as I write this. I am aware that there are countless homeless people struggling every single day. Due to this, I think it is purely selfish to waste the great life that you have been given. So, make the most out of your gift of time!

I am not saying you should never take a break. However, people sometimes take such long breaks that they waste time and then start complaining about not having enough time. Seize every opening of time that you have. Get right with your time!

How dedicated will you be?

The No. 1 thing that will give you an advantage over everybody else costs nothing: It's your will to succeed.

And you have to consider achieving this goal critical to your very existence and survival. Motivational speaker Eric Thomas famously said, "When you want to succeed as bad as you want to breathe, you will be successful."

Being dedicated means putting your one goal ahead of all the hundreds of other things. It means putting it ahead of the need for food, even the need for water when you are thirsty.

There is no point in being "kind of." The rest of society is "kind-of" dedicated to what they do. If you think being like the rest of society is fine, then you shouldn't be reading this. You are reading this because you want to be better. You want to be dedicated and see results. Choose all or nothing.

Why people say don't focus on the money and how you should interpret that

When people keep their eye on the money more

than what they are doing and why they are doing it, they are focusing on the money too much. Focus on the money after what you are working to achieve. Money is important, but don't let it affect the vision of what you are doing. Focus on the numbers and keep track of where you are in business, so that you know how to progress. However, don't direct your attention on the money more than on the actual business.

I look at money as a measurement of your progress in business. It shows how much you have helped people and added value to the world. For example, If you help a million people through a product, and each pays you ten bucks for what you did, you make ten million dollars. To achieve this, you would have to focus on helping the ten million people. The money is just a measurement of how many people you helped and how much help you gave each of them. It's simple! Make sense?

The most simple answer on how to be wealthy

There is a very, very simple answer on how to become wealthy. People ask how they can become millionaires, or even billionaires. What do you think? Is it hard work, is it timing, or is it just shear dedication? Well, you should certainly have all of these traits. However, there exists an answer far simpler and straight-forward than any of those.

So, you want to become a millionaire? Help a

million people. You want to be a billionaire? Impact the lives of a billion people. Simple! Take a step back and think about how much value you are giving to people and how much of a difference you want to make. That is how much money you will earn. It is not always about how hard you work, but amount how much you produce and provide for the world.

For example, founder of Amazon, Jeff Bezos, has accumulated huge amounts of wealth through Amazon. There are some people who might say things like he doesn't deserve that much! You may or may not like Amazon, but I say he deserves every penny he made. It is not an opinion, but a fact. The fact that he has provided convenience to millions of people, means that he deserves all the money he has made. People will not support a business unless they can get a lot of value and benefits from it. Jeff Bezos has done this for millions of lives, so he deserves what he gets because people have continually provided business to him!

To explain further, if you want to be a millionaire, provide $100 worth of value to ten thousand people. You'll make a million dollars. Remember, it is not necessarily about how hard you work, but how much you help people in total that will determine how much you get.

Chapter three

FINDING WAYS AROUND PROBLEMS

Turn those problems into benefits

One of the biggest initial business challenges for me has been being under the age of 18. I couldn't do some of the things I wanted to do being a kid, and additionally, one still in school. Even though I may have missed out on opportunities and advantages because of my age, I don't complain; I do something.

For instance, when a potential buyer expressed interest in one of my paintings that was on display in a gallery, I was advised to lower my price because I was so young. But after talking it over with my parents, I told the gallery owner that if other artists of equal quality work were selling for a higher price, why should I lower my price just because I was so young? The very nice owner agreed, and was surprised when my painting sold for 25 percent over the initial price.

Many artists depend on or use galleries to promote them and their work. This is where I have taken a slightly different path as a kid. I have not "worked" for a gallery. Instead, I have built my own network of buyers who support my art. So far, I get my own clients about 90 percent of the time. I do commissions or sell by myself. In the future, I might go to galleries for the large customer base they possess, but for now, I rarely pay commissions to other people or galleries.

To build a network, I reached out to local organizations to promote me. I made a website and carved a path for myself. I have made sure I get people talking about me. I have become not just an artist, but also an entrepreneur!

I believe there is always a solution. Just look at all the great figures in history who have achieved the impossible: Martin Luther King, Gandhi, Nelson Mandela, Mother Teresa, Abraham Lincoln, and many more heroes show us that there always lies a way in the midst of the impossible. Keep searching.

When I hit roadblocks, I realized I just had to use what I had. Books advised that your family and friends can be your best support when starting a business. Unfortunately, I barely have family here, as most of them live in India, where my parents are from. I also wasn't someone who had a ton of friends at the time. But this pushed me to look further for solutions.

I realize that overcoming these hurdles taught me a lot more than if someone had just set me up in business. I didn't wait for someone to come to me and show me exactly how to do it all step-by-step. I searched relentlessly for answers. I read several dozens of books and watched hundreds of hours of YouTube videos to teach and educate myself.

Now I have family members in India who are my customers. So my initial complaint about not having family in Chicago turned into an advantage, because I can honestly say my business is international!

Get past those limitations of being a kid if you are one

One of the major challenges of being a young entrepreneur under eighteen is getting past the struggles of, well, being a kid. For all the support my family now offers, initially they were a source of discouragement and doubt.

I had to prove to my parents that I could monetize my art and other hobbies or ideas. Once you get past the initial hurdles, opportunities and rewards flow in. The great thing is, if you keep your head down and focus on the task, you will often get more of a reward than you can even imagine.

The hard part comes when you face the challenge of staying motivated. When you are in that low spot, you become narrow-minded about the future. That results in fear because your vision shrinks and you feel lost.

And there are so many success stories being told on social media and elsewhere, that you can become discouraged when you compare what you've accomplished to the many achievements of others. Think more about the reward, and do not view any mountain as so high it scares you to even take the first step. Focus on your goal and keep pushing, while having the right balance of inspiration and dreams.

Work toward your goals and respect will follow

Sometimes the best way to get people to take you seriously is to prove them wrong. But don't work hard just for that reason. Work because you want to create something and work because you want to, then you will rise above others without even realizing it.

It wasn't too long ago that I was hoping to make money selling paintings at art shows and fairs. I had huge business potential with my artistic talents that I had been developing on my own. I had so much potential sitting right there that I could be using to stand out from the crowd. One summer I decided that I was going to commit to doing professional paintings, and managed to finish a painting every day.

That same summer, my art skills improved more in two months than they had in six years of merely dabbling in art.

People and my parents would ask me, what will

make your college application stand out? I remember being compared to other kids who were winning tennis matches or participating in state robotic championships.

Previously I had counted on the usual couple sports and playing the violin to show that I had extracurricular activities. But the magic happened when I focused on my art, which I really enjoy. From selling a painting in an art gallery, to getting that first commission, to building my website, I had gained a uniqueness that impressed people everywhere.

When people asked me what my "stand out" factor would be for college, I pointed to my website and handed them my business card.

Then I just watched their jaws drop.

Chapter four

MAKE IT HAPPEN

Decide to get it done

Many people keep wanting results but they just never make things happen.

For me, writing this book is one example of pushing through to make something happen. After my friend suggested that I write a book, I just let the thought percolate for at least a month. Then I began feeling guilty about not starting the book, and something inside me just kept telling me to put all my thoughts into words.

In a sense, I was guilty of not "making it happen" right away. But for some reason I suddenly committed to the book. Every day, even during school, I came in thirty minutes early to write. Sitting alone during lunch, I was writing. When school ended for the summer, my writing and other business productivity skyrocketed. The very first week of summer, I was writing twelve pages a day. No excuses. No debate.

You know you are on the right track when your results are more than what you expect. People kept telling me I should stop worrying about money, and start acting like a normal kid. I heard them, and then decided what to ignore and what to take in. The result was I was happier and got more done. I couldn't believe where I was at after the first week of seriously writing. And now I see this mindset working in other areas of my life.

For example: When I first wanted to set up a website for one of my business, I kept asking my parents to help me. At the time, I had no idea how to set up a website and connect it to a domain. I didn't even know what a domain was. I just wanted to find out how to make a real website with a ".com."

For several months my parents just kept saying they were busy and "I'll think about it." I kept getting more and more eager as time went by. I finally told myself, "If I don't do this, no one will."

The next day I finished the whole website by myself, thanks to my most reliable resource, YouTube. I couldn't believe my results. Again, I exceeded my own expectations. My "just make it happen" thinking helped convince my parents to pay for everything without more than ten minutes of "I'll think about it and let you know." It's a good example of your work ethic and passion spreading to others.

My thinking went from what I wanted to do to

how I would do it. Next, I just worked to get it done. Before I knew it, I was asking myself, where did that website just appear from? This is what you'll be asking yourself when you just make it happen.

Don't spend too much time thinking about what you're going to do. Time is precious. I wasted a month thinking about making my business cards. To be honest, I didn't really even think. I actually just wasted lots of time.

Now I don't waste time, because I realize that it takes only a few minutes to complete simple tasks. I drew up my design in a minute, found a printing company online and ordered a hundred business cards. The next day, there they were right at my doorstep!

The two things that I had wasted so much time thinking about -- a website and business cards -- are what got me many more sales.

Yes, you should think about things before you take action, but not to the point where you are wasting time. Don't procrastinate!!

Work like a robot

The first time people hear me say "Work like a robot," they quickly recoil, saying that people aren't robots, and we should not think that way.

But what I mean by working like a robot is not letting emotions, hunger or tiredness get in your way. The result will be that you will use 100 percent of your potential. Your body will tell you when it is time to eat or sleep. Don't let your mind make decisions for you. Robots do not think about anything more than what they are programmed to do. Use less of your brain when you actually do the work. Reserve time to think about what to do, and then focus only on action to get things done.

When a robot is programmed, a lot of thinking goes into that first step. After it is programmed, however, the robot simply gets to work, doing what it's programmed to do. Similarly, program yourself in one step, and then get to work.

You might ask, shouldn't I also be thinking smart while working? The answer is yes. Now, the process isn't as discrete as I may make it sound. It is not as if you don't even use your brain when you work. You work intelligently, but you don't ponder other thoughts while working. You really focus getting things done. Take time to make up your mind, and take time to get things done. So in a broad perspective, the process is: Think, work, think, work, and so on. Work, reflect on your work, come up with new ideas, and work more.

If you don't focus on working, you start generating things like fear, disappointment, doubt, and sadness. These things slow you down, and your focus goes downhill. Also, when you face failure, it can lower your confidence. So: Act like a robot. Recharge and work like nothing happened.

I know it is easy to say, but not so easy to do, but just imagine yourself as a machine and work.

Stop worrying

In my high school honors science class, I kept getting bad grades on tests no matter how hard I tried. I kept getting more and more discouraged. Meanwhile, my teacher was telling me that I should be getting motivated by these bad results. But I kept asking myself, how in the world am I supposed to get motivated by failure, when the negativity just leads to more negativity?

I realized it was because the negativity, failure, and worry were being reinforced. As soon as I managed to get my first A, I then got consecutive A's. I realized that I simply needed to concentrate on the next grade and just do the work.

So don't worry too much if you can't stay focused. The more you worry about something, the less you can get done. The best way to stop worrying about things is to keep busy and think about positive results, while keeping your eye on the goal. That way you don't have time for worrying or even to think about worrying.

Here's the main point: Keep busy and focus on the results you want. And stop with the worrying!

Chapter five

VISUALIZE YOUR GOAL

Why maintaining a vision is important

Being a true visionary means you are seeing your accomplishments before they become reality. And picturing your future is an essential part of creating.

I had been thinking about how to get into e-commerce, and came up with the idea of creating little handmade wooden bookmarks featuring small paintings and designs on them. It would be an extension of my art business.

There were some problems I had to deal with, like finding wood that would be sturdy, yet thin enough to serve as a bookmark. After exploring my options, I quickly found the exact kind of rich walnut I was looking for. That same day, I made my first bookmark.

The next day I watched YouTube videos on how to create an online store on Etsy.com. Then I persuaded my parents to help me create a store on the site. The result: I started getting orders from different parts of the country! I was amazed how fast I could craft my imagination into a tangible form!

Think about your hobbies or something you have a passion for. Is there a vision you have for these interests? If so, get to work and make that vision a reality. Remember: You must persevere!

How to be a successful visionary

One summer I went to a Yanni concert that took place right on the 25th anniversary of a previous concert the musician had performed at the Acropolis in Greece. Yanni talked about all the determination it took to stage a concert at the ancient Greek site. He left the audience with an impactful message about following your dreams. Despite what others thought was impossible, he just focused on his vision. For him, the very successful concert was a new beginning.

So how do you get from where you are to where you want to be? See your goals ahead of time. In fact, write a one-page letter describing yourself in the third person. Write about who you want to be in one month, one year, or five years. Then commit to doing whatever you need to in order to become that person.

This is not just about where you want to be

financially; it is about where you want to be in all aspects of yourself. Maybe you would like to be friendlier and happier. You can even write about your daily routines. Go into as much detail as you can.

Envisioning your future self and committing that vision to paper can help you map out the steps needed to become the person you want to be.

Once you have your plan, it's critical that you stick to it. I can't stress that enough, because if you are all over the place, you will never become that future successful self.

You don't want to dream a little more than everybody else, you want to dream a lot more. You must have a vision stronger than anyone else! It is like having extremely talented and smart students in a room, but no teacher to tell them how to use their intelligence to create an extraordinary future.

A strong vision paired with hard work can produce lightning!

Dreaming both big and small

I was always just dreaming about publicizing my art business. I knew what I needed to do, but I kept wasting time and making excuses instead.

One idea I had was to set up my easel outdoors in a busy area. My plan was that when people stopped to see what I was doing, I could hand out my business card. Maybe out of all the people, I could get one person to actually contact me. It was a very time-consuming and tedious plan. And it was too small.

When I finally decided to get serious about my next step, I went looking for someone who knew many people in the art world. That led me to an art gallery, where I got some of the exposure I wanted.

Then I connected with a local community Facebook group that had a huge number of people in it. They offered to give a shout-out to me, and I decided that this was perfect. In the first few minutes of my post, I had likes pouring in. I couldn't believe the rate. On that same day, I got an email. The next day, I closed a deal and got a painting sold! Making a plan and following through on my steps had paid off.

It's good to dream big. However, you have to make sure you don't get lost in a dreamy world where you don't accomplish anything. Not enough people tell you that you should also focus on the short-term in addition to the long-term.

People who divide up their goals and know exactly how to achieve them will be the ones who succeed. Each day matters. Ask yourself if you are setting your goals high and know how to get there, or are you setting your goals high and just dreaming about them?

Through my years of doing oil painting, one of the biggest things I learned was to step back from the canvas every once in a while to look at what I had done instead of always focusing on the details. I learned to use different angles of vision. The same exact approach works in life.

You need to try to view what you are doing from different perspectives.

Stepping back will help you see yourself as others see you. It will ensure that you are on the right course, and that you aren't seeing life from just your own point of view.

Don't dream too big, and don't dream too small. You need to find that sweet spot. It is like if you look at something from too far away, it's impossible to see. But if you are too close, it's impossible to even make out what it is.

The two states of mind you must balance

An issue I sometimes face in entrepreneurship is knowing when to switch from focused and calm to energized and motivated. It can be tough to transition between these two states of mind. I've learned how to better manage this transition, and realize that there is a time and a place for both of these mindsets.

For example, when you go to the library, it is nice and quiet. It is a good place to get work done. When you are calm and focused, you know what to do, and you can make things happen.

However, people also need to be pumped and ready to go every morning. I would watch inspiring videos in the mornings and maybe go for a bike ride while listening to some energizing music. I would get all excited for the day, but then my mind would start to wander and I wouldn't be able to settle down and get work done. I needed to find the right balance of these two states of mind and work on how to transition quickly from inspired and excited to calm and focused.

It's an ongoing struggle, and I now carefully think what the moment calls for. You need to be aware of which one to have and when. Balancing these properly leads to maximum productivity.

Chapter six

SELLING ADVICE FOR NEWBIES OF ALL AGES

Selling for the first time can be quite intimidating, especially when it comes to e-commerce, where a majority of selling is taking place. People are cutting out the middleman, and brick and mortar stores are feeling the pressure. It is very easy to open up your own store these days. The only hard part is learning how everything works.

Why people think things are hard when they do them for the first time

Doing something you've never done before can make you nervous and afraid. People worry about what will happen before even taking that first step.

I say that you should focus on making things happen. Don't dwell on the "might be" problems before you act. Fear isn't tangible; it's a mindset. It's the trick your mind plays on you that stops you from doing new things. Confronting fear is part of the steep slope you must climb toward starting your business.

Putting in the effort to learn the mechanics of how things work pays off in better results. You can't misplace knowledge. It's right there in your brain, waiting to help you get the results you want. With time, your knowledge can yield results with little effort on your part.

Don't fear failure -- there will always be a way

People complain about not being able to start their own business because they don't have a backup plan in case things go wrong. For example, some people do not have family in America, which means they have no support system if they fail.

Get to know the consequences but don't fear them. If you become homeless and broke, do not fear that. When you are at rock bottom, there is only one way left to go, and that's up! That is quite extreme, but see the point here. If you keep complaining about not being able to do the things because you don't have a backup plan, you are letting fear put a roadblock in your path.

If you have a true desire to succeed and will to do whatever it takes, you will be willing to overcome those fears and roadblocks. You should be open to fail as much as you succeed. So, if you want mega-success, you should be okay with mega-failure.

Let people such as Nelson Mandela inspire you. He found his way out of one of the most brutal jails in South Africa to become president of his country. He and other similar heroes confronted their fears and used their missions in life as shields against the consequences of taking action.

Now let's start selling

I am going to throw some straight-to-the-point information at you now. You have the product and you need to sell it.

I am not going to talk so much about brick and mortar retail or television shopping networks, and other such techniques, simply because that is not my space. Through my experience, though, I will talk about the following. The options of selling range from going door to door to selling online. If you are like me, you mainly just interact with your customers face to face and close big deals with each individual customer instead of focusing on volume. For the options I talk about in this chapter, each has its advantages and I recommend you do both. Here's why. Sometimes, you don't need any "platforms" to get started; just reaching out to people and powerful networking can get you those first customers. However, there are significant benefits to doing e-commerce, online advertising, and using other similar techniques.

hv

Selling online

An online presence has quite a lot of potential and space for growth. It's a place for highly expandable businesses. You don't want to start at too high a level or stay small either. And you don't want to make big mistakes. It depends where you are regarding your e-commerce game.

I don't recommend starting out by creating your own website if you are not confident in marketing it, because getting a customer base becomes solely your responsibility. In contrast, sites such as Ebay and Amazon already have millions of shoppers who are constantly browsing. It is easier to advertise and start out. This chapter is for e-commerce beginners, so we'll take it easy.

The first step: Figure out what you are selling. I am going to assume it is a product. Even if it is a service, you can turn it into a product to sell online. For example, teaching someone is a service. But if you turn those instructions into a video and put it on a DVD, you now have a product. Turning a service into a product is a great way to expand a business.

Check out websites that show you how to sell and guide you through the process. This guidance will prepare you for going professional.

As tempting as it might be to go big quickly, it's better to test the waters first. So before going to major sites such as Amazon, start with specialized smaller sites like Esty.com, which give you flexibility and room for mistakes.

Etsy is the No. 1 site for kids and adults who want to start selling but don't want to be bogged down with work and a full-time commitment.

There are a lot of things I like about Etsy, which is great for absolute beginners when it comes to e-commerce. First, kids are encouraged to participate on the site. You just need to have a parent own the account. Once you get signed up, you can own and operate the business. The site walks people through the decision-making process, from those with no idea of what to do to those who are hoping to make hundreds to thousands of dollars.

Sellers have so much flexibility and you can virtually sell anything. There is very little upfront cost, and I mean very little. The price for listing a product is literally in cents. You can resell or make anything you want and list it on Etsy.

When someone orders your product, the money is transferred to your bank account electronically, and you receive a notification to ship your order via email or on etsy.com. Just package the order and ship it by dropping it off at the post office. There are even step-by-step videos on the site. (More details are available on etsy.com.)

When it comes to e-commerce, you need to decide how much time you want to dedicate to selling. But if you are looking to really win at e-commerce, you shouldn't be asking yourself how much time and effort you are willing to commit. You need to be all in.

If you are a kid, you have commitments to school and extracurricular activities, of course. But, you should be willing to commit 100 percent of your free time to e-commerce if you do it. This should be something that excites you and interests you, otherwise your sales will suffer. Underperforming right after starting an online business is out of the question. That is frankly worse than not even doing business at all. Be all in or don't waste your time setting something up.

You also need to determine your exact niche, regarding which websites are best for you. Examples of niches are food, fashion, crafts, art and so on. Once you determine your niche, see if the website you are thinking of using is successful at selling in that area. For example, for art you might want to think about fineartamerica.com or other similar sites.

Starting with these websites means you can begin selling online while you are still figuring things out. Nonetheless, be prepared to face some challenges. Luckily, you can always turn to YouTube, Google and other online resources for help.

And here's another tip: Don't wait for people to find your products online. I have seen beginners do this and then they complain that it can take weeks or months until they get their first order. Spread the word yourself among your friends and family! Once you start getting sales from these people, your product will move up in the search results and strangers will start finding and buying your product. Keep driving your sales forward by talking to people and working. If you just sit back, you won't see results.

Even if you don't succeed, you can learn a lot

from trying e-commerce. I dropped out of my little e-commerce venture because I wanted to focus my time and energy on another business that was important to me. But operating the online shop taught me quite a good bit.

Shopify and drop-shipping

It's a common misconception that you need your own products to have an online business or store. Shopify, an online platform used to create a store, and drop-shipping, where packages are shipped directly from a manufacturer, are a great way to do e-commerce without having to deal with inventory or investing lots of upfront money. It is yielding many success stories on the internet and has a lot of potential.

With Shopify, you are somewhat like the middle man. You set up an online store that sells specific products; your store can specialize in things like sports gear or maybe household items for instance. You create the website, or online store, and then find inventory to sell via your store. The great thing is, you don't have to make your own products.

You can go to sites like AliExpress, an online Chinese retail service, and sell its products in your online store. You mark the price up and sell with a profit. When the person buys from your store, you simply place their order on AliExpress, and AliExpress ships that product to the buyer. That way you don't hold inventory. People don't usually buy directly from the company; they buy from a specialized and well-known store. Your online store's niche can be directly targeted to customers on sites like Facebook.

You could also reach out to social media influencers on Youtube or Instagram to promote your products, and then direct customers to your website. It is a process full of many hurdles, but can yield large sums of money if done right.

Shopify and their apps are making things easier than ever for anybody to sell online. Keep in mind that since you are not manufacturing the products, but simply creating a better channel to sell them through, you must become good at selling and marketing. Besides, it is a skill that will never go waste.

The real purpose of door- to door sales

My first door-to-door experience was selling handcrafted candles I made at home when I was in the 2nd or 3rd grade. I made my own price tags out of cut-out paper, and bought candle wax, a few jars, some wicks, fragrance and some dye from a Michaels craft store. I would heat the wax in the microwave and hand-pour each candle. Part of the appeal of the candles was that they were handmade by a kid. People loved them. I sold them to teachers as well as door to door.

My goal was to just make some pocket money, and looking back I would say it was a pretty successful business. It was the first time I made money other than being paid to do household chores.

You might ask, if I have all these ways to sell online, why bother with traditional door-to-door sales? The answer: for the valuable lessons that such selling offers. There is no better way to learn how to talk, interact with people, and close deals while also growing a thick skin.

The concept is simple: Someone answers your knock on the door and you have just a few minutes to give your presentation. That sure beats those presentations you have to do in school! And door-to-door sales can have huge rewards. It is the perfect loop. You get better and better, and then you make your first sale! Bam! Talk about immediate positive feedback!

Of course, you have to overcome the fear of knocking on a door for the first time, not knowing who will be there and what their reaction will be. You will most likely face many rejections and get doors slammed in your face. (Pay attention to those No Soliciting signs.) That's just part of the deal though. It's what makes you stronger, and it's why door to door selling is so valuable.

A few of the many homes you approach are bound to buy something. And if you're a kid, you have the advantage of being able to mount a charm offensive, which motivates people to buy from you. It's just a matter of knocking on as many doors as you can.

After a day of selling door to door, write down what you learned and what you had problems with. Take note of which sales pitches worked and which ones didn't. Improve on what you think you did wrong. Always be learning while you sell. Read books on selling; check out what sales experts have to say. The next time you go out selling door to door, use what you learned. Keep doing this and you will see results. Once you get the results, just keep working.

Sometimes you just have to get yourself in front of people rather than hope they notice you. The great thing is that, there is an abundance of houses. You can never run out of customers, you can just run out of your own will to sell.

As for my handcrafted candle business, I would approach it a lot differently now. But that just shows that I learned from it!

Passion: To pursue or not to pursue

Some successful people tell you not to follow your passion. I believe that this is true to a certain extent, even though my business arose out of my passion.

You have to make sure your business model is scalable and is something that draws customers. For this reason, you have to be careful when trying to monetize your passion. Make sure your passion has the potential to yield success. It is so much easier to stay committed if you are passionate about your work and not simply looking for a big payout as your goal.

I think you should know why you are pursuing a goal, what you are doing to achieve that goal, and what results you are hoping for. Money is important, but it shouldn't be the primary driver. Maximizing your passion and your commitment to work can yield big dividends.

Chapter seven

PACKAGING

It speaks volumes

Packaging says a lot about you without uttering a single word.

One time I bought some muffins from a new baking business in my neighborhood. The muffins arrived in a very sloppy box with crushed business cards. Even though the muffins were delicious, the packaging said "blah." When I asked the owner about the packaging, they said they didn't have the resources to upgrade their packaging.

But the packaging should have reflected the care that went into the baking.

As for the baker's business card, there are online companies that print as many as a hundred business cards for just $4.99. My best friend told me once, "Your business card is like a firm handshake", and that could never be closer to the truth. Instead of presenting a cheaply made card that wasn't even cut straight, it would have been better to just have spent five dollars to show the customer that the business was professional.

Nice packaging doesn't have to be expensive; it just takes some research. If you can't find something to fit your budget, make your packaging yourself, but make it good! Your guiding principle should be to exceed customers' expectations, not underwhelm them.

All your extra things like packaging, business cards, etc, do a lot more than you might think they do. They alone, can be your salespeople when you are not selling. Cut profits if you have to, because you want to invest for the long-term. Create a good impression on the customer with your packaging. So, don't compromise on them!

The three degrees of packaging

If you are buying toilet paper from Walmart, you don't expect to see lovely packaging. Shrink-wrap works just fine. The bigger concerns are whether the toilet paper is soft and durable.

But if you are looking to splurge on an expensive bottle of perfume, you expect more: a beautiful box and a carefully designed bottle holding a lovely scent.

Packaging should convey information about the product, which can occupy any one of three broad categories: tech, luxury and consumer goods. And each category has its own packaging personality.

Tech

The best kind of packaging when it comes to technology, usually combines sophistication and simplicity.

Apple products offer one of the best examples of this. Steve Jobs insisted that the parts you don't see be just as perfect as the parts you do see. The result of his vision are computers with a flawless finished back and front without any clutter of cheap plastic.

The smooth metal back of the iPod matches the sleek white Apple box. And those boxes slide open with a precision and sophistication that enhance the buyer's experience. Shopping bags are made of thicker paper with textured white material. Apple keeps it simple while maintaining its unique identity among other tech products.

The quality packaging is in keeping with the excitement the shopper feels about owning the product inside. It's all part of exceeding customers' expectations.

Luxury/gift

Packaging luxury and gift items sits right in my wheelhouse.

I think of my paintings as a journey, and when the journey ends with the painting in the client's hands, I want that moment to be special, as special as the painting itself.

I'm very particular about how I package each

painting, and always include a personal note or letter. Every client to date has complimented me on my packaging. Some have even insisted on paying me more than the asking price just because of the experience I have them!

Instead of reducing price, increase the value, as entrepreneur Grant Cardone says.

Louis Vuitton distinguishes itself by using a leather band to wrap around its boxes. Luxury watchmaker Patek Phillipe uses leather envelopes for its receipts. When your watches sell for anywhere between $30,000 and $11 million, the leather receipt holder wraps up the transaction with a touch of class.

Packaging sends a powerful message about the quality of what's inside. Don't just say something is luxurious, show it! Walk the talk by packaging your products correctly. Another example of packaging detail: Gucci provides cloth silica gel pouches instead of the traditional paper ones. Who would think of adding detail to the packaging of silica gel? You need to focus on details just like this to show that you mean serious business!

Entrepreneur Tai Lopez says "Turn everything you touch into gold." I've done this with how I package my paintings, and it sure has paid off!

Consumer goods

Packaging consumer goods is about having the package show what the product can do and how it will help the customer. The package should also be eye-catching. Spending more on consumer goods packaging will not necessarily get you more customers. It is more about the design than quality.

Choosing the right colors and type fonts are the essentials of successful consumer goods packaging. Colors can convey a message about a product. For instance, blue signifies security and trust, which is why banks often use blue.

Green, which is the easiest color for the eye to process, is about relaxation. Yellow is optimistic and cheerful.

Purple is soothing; pink is playful and can be used to show something is for females.

Red and orange are seen as aggressive and striking; they get attention. They also portray the product as powerful and exciting. The cover of this book uses red and orange to draw readers' eyes to the promise that reading this book can bring change to your life.

How words are arranged, the type, size, and choice of fonts can play up certain messages and draw a customer's eye closer. Bigger, bolder type demands attention; smaller, subdued type quietly offers details.

Choose the right words that speak for the product and explain what it does. Be concise -- you don't want to overwhelm the packaging with too many words.

Packaging on a consumer good can be the sole reason that it sells. It can be the make-or-break point of a customers decision. So get it right the first time!

Chapter eight

HOW TO GET AND KEEP YOUR FIRST CUSTOMERS

Talk about your business everywhere you go

Many people make the mistake of spending money on advertising and do everything they can online, but never talk about their business to friends and people they meet.

Talking to your friends about your business doesn't mean you are soliciting them. You are merely sharing what you are up to and what is going on with you.

When you walk into a room full of strangers, most of the time there is a way to leave that room with some, if not all, of the people knowing about your business. A great lesson I learned from my mentors on youtube, was that whether you are liked or disliked, I think it is better for people to know about you than to just be an unknown.

This is how you build your network. In the process, you might discover, as I did, that you have been transformed from an introvert into an extrovert.

You will learn how to approach people, make conversation and leave them knowing all about who you are. I really started practicing this skill at school. Why school? It was a big network of people already present around me. Most of my day spent was at school, so why not tell people about my businesses?

One of the first times I realized the value of this was when I got to class one day and saw a new substitute teacher in the room. I decided that I would find a way to make a connection with that teacher and give her one of my business cards before the class was over. I wanted to make sure she knew who I was.

My opportunity came when I found out she spoke French and Spanish. That led to conversation about Paris, the Louvre and art. Voila! I handed her my card.

Be open to getting to know people. Find out what they are interested in. When it feels natural, bring up your interests and see what happens from there.

It is much easier now to talk about myself when people say "tell me about yourself" than it was just a year ago.

Again, this is just one of the benefits of starting your own business. You become so much better at social skills.

Always be expanding your social interface

When someone asks you if you know a lot of people, you should be able to say yes -- a huge amount!

Many people prefer to have a few, close friends. And this works, but you should also make sure that you know a lot of people and that a lot of people know you.

If your social skills are weak, improve them. Of course, not everyone is going to be a close friend. But come on, there are more than seven billion people on this planet. You don't have to become close friends with them all, but you can make a lot of acquaintances.

Ask people you meet about their personal interests. Listen to what they say and get to know them. Spend time with them and you can call them your friends, or at least acquaintances. You can get many benefits from influencing and making an impact on one friend, but imagine influencing a hundred friends.

If you really don't like someone and they are not a good person to be around, just move on. All I am saying is that you should learn to develop connections with the people you meet, and always build your network.

Even if you see no reason to acquire friends, do it anyway. If you are not interested in being a more social person, do it anyway. When you need help, your connections will help you out or find opportunities for you. Also if you are selling online, you can get your first sales and reviews by just working the social network you have made for yourself.

But remember: It's important to be genuine and sincere with your friends. Send out kindness and it will come back to you. These people can be your first customers. They can offer solutions to problems you face in business. They also can simply be friends you like to be with.

Just remember that out of a large number of people you connect with, there will always be those few special people who will be genuine toward you and really offer you some immense opportunities. With my business, I have simply made the effort to get to know everybody everywhere I go, and out of those many people, a few of them have given me invaluable opportunities.

It is also how I have managed to scale the number of clients in my own business without much external assistance or any unnecessary complications. You don't have to make a close relationship with every single person. Just make sure they know you and you know them!

Being an introvert is NOT an excuse

If you consider yourself an introvert, don't think you are at a disadvantage. Bill Gates and Albert Einstein were both introverts.

I consider myself an introvert, although I have pushed myself toward being more extroverted. I speak more naturally with the people I know than the people I don't know. Introverts are reserved and quiet. They also can be careful people who can focus and make wise decisions. The world sometimes puts negative connotations on introverts. If you are an introvert, you can be just as successful as those extroverts who enjoy being the center of attention.

My tips for if you want to be more outgoing than you are

If you are like me, you have no problem talking to people you know well. The issue is meeting people for the first time.

My suggestion: Pretend the new people you meet are people you already know. Don't worry so much about saying the wrong thing. Just talk to them like they already know you and like you.

Sometimes when people are shy or too quiet, other people avoid them and don't engage in conversation, thinking that the shy person wants to be left alone or isn't interested in talking to them.

Be friendly enough in order to create a good first impression, and encourage others to tell you about themselves.

How to present your products or services to people and ask for sales

Let's say you now have the friends and the power base to work from. How do you present your products and get people to buy them?

First: Don't be afraid to talk about your business with people. Before you do anything, make sure people know about you. Try to fit it into conversations. Be creative. If you don't see a spot to talk about your business in a conversation, come up with a way to just tell them about it straight out.

For example, I have come up to quite a few people and just asked how they are doing, and then say I am doing well, and then tell them what I have been up to. Most of the time, you will have to initiate conversations to get your friends and the people you know to be your first customers.

A good example of a conversation starter is to start talking about business right before the weekend, when people are usually asking if you have plans. This is the perfect chance to make your indirect little sales pitch. Some of you may say this is wrong or that you should never sell to your friends. How else do you start then? Aren't your friends there to help you?

Your first customers are the most important and hard to get. They are the ones who will get you other customers and talk about you after their experiences. This is why working your network is a great place to start.

Get people talking about you

Make sure you are committed to your business before you start pushing to get the word out. If you are truly committed, go for it!

Start by giving your first customers an unforgettable experience. You'll be on your way to being the talk of the town. Remember to exceed expectations.

If you don't have a large network to work with, start with what you have. Ask your small circle of friends to tell others they know about you. Reach out to groups and organizations on social media. Pitch yourself to local media; don't wait until people tell you that you are newsworthy.

Also, remember that you don't need to have your audience already built. You can actually use others to promote you. Before I started my art business, my mom would hang my paintings and art in her office, with no intention of selling or advertising my work. But there were always people passing by her office, and my work got noticed. That low-key display by my mom of my work would lead to my first commission. The desk at the office already had its own "audience". The employees there would be the potential customers. I didn't need be an influencer on social media just to get my first commission. It was just because of that simple act.

And remember the old slogan: Advertising doesn't cost; it pays.

What it means to make each experience personal

Making an experience personal doesn't always mean writing a personal letter, or having your customer's name printed, embroidered or painted on the product.

Making an experience personal means valuing all your customers, from the big spender to the not-so-big spender. This means adapting to the customer's needs. It means helping the customer find what is right for them, instead of what you think will make you the most money for yourself.

When you offer personalized service, it makes people feel good. That is why people are willing to pay so much more money for custom items.

Lamborghini makes special edition cars that skyrocket in value. People sometimes pay whatever it takes because they value the fact that they will be the one of few who owns the Lamborghini.

So think about making your interactions with each client special in some way.

My family and I were on the receiving end of excellent customer service on a gift-buying trip to Macy's. We were deciding between a handbag and some perfume when we asked a sales associate in the perfume section for her opinion.

Only after a series of thoughtful questions -- Who was the gift for? What was the occasion? How old was the recipient? -- did she recommend the perfume. Yes, she was a perfume salesperson, but she also had spent a lot of time with us, making sure we made the right choice and offering good reasons for the purchase.

It was customer service and personal attention at its best.

Treat all your customers or even potential customers like they are ready to buy your products or services.

Remember all that talk on visualizing your goal? That's the kind of mindset you need in order to successfully sell your product to a potential customer.

Obviously, not every customer will buy from you. But if you start by treating everyone as though they are your prime client, you can turn some of those "maybe's" into "sold!"

Sure, you could waste time on a customer who doesn't buy from you despite your best efforts. But that's not as bad as losing a sale because you didn't spend enough time with the potential buyer.

Eventually you can develop a sense of who is likely to buy from you. Treat everyone well, and be gracious even when you know you aren't going to get a sale.

Obviously you will want to focus more intently on those who appear more serious about your product. When you start to narrow down customers, start to increase the time and attention you give to that "more-likely-to-be" customer.

Don't judge potential customers by their appearance or how they talk. Treat everyone with respect. You never know what your best customer is going to look like. There is a great story I once came across about the consequences of judging your customers negatively. It goes like this...

An Indian Maharaja (king), named Jai Singh, had come to visit London. He was strolling along the streets in his casual attire when he came across a Rolls-Royce dealership. He went in to inquire about the cars. The salesman took one look at him and judged him as a poor Indian who couldn't afford anything. The salesman discriminated against him and rudely walked him out of the showroom. It was certainly quite an insult to royalty!

The Maharaja went back to his hotel room the same day and ordered his servants to tell the same exact showroom that the Maharaja of Alwar was visiting. After hearing this, the showroom rolled out the red carpet and devoted all their attention and time to that same king, now knowing he was part of royalty. The maharaja bought all six cars in the showroom that day, and transported them to Alwar, India, where he ruled.

The king took the same Rolls-Royces that he had bought and ordered his city's municipal department to use them as waste transporters and waste collecting vehicles around the city. As soon as people took notice of Rolls- Royces being used to collect garbage, word spread rapidly. Those who once proudly drove their Rolls-Royces on the streets, were embarrassed to withhold such a name. Rolls-Royce's sales quickly plummeted.

Much later, did Rolls-Royce finally realize the incident that happened. The company sent the maharaja a telegram with an apology, and six more Rolls-Royces for free.

It is quite a story! And, it just goes to show what a long way customer service can go. So never judge a customer for anything. Treat everybody equally like they are your prime, type A customers. Your kindness will come back around to you and benefit you much in business. But remember, do the opposite, and one bad customer experience can go a long way too!

What I've seen as a result of giving people as much value as you can

Many entrepreneurs will tell you this: When you give extra value to people, you often get even more in return.

When I asked people how much I should be selling my artwork for, they told me that I should carefully divide up all the hours I spent on my paintings and charge according to a formula. They told me I should come up with a reasonable and steady rate for my clients. But I decided to just pour my heart into my work and not worry so much about the specific hours I was investing.

I wanted to make myself stand out by providing extra services, even when customers didn't want to pay a lot for what I was selling. There have been many times where I have done my best for people and not even thought about how many hours I worked. One person who initially told me he would be cheap and that my asking price was too high, ended up paying me 30 percent more than what I asked for!

My very first customer commissioned a painting from me without ever even meeting me. He believed I could do the painting for him based on other works of mine that he had seen. When I started that first painting, I put my heart into it.

I credit this person, who would go on to become one of my best friends, and the spark that launched my art business. After making him a very happy customer with that first commission, he requested a second painting several months later.

I knew this one had to be exceptional, from the painting to the packaging. I went so far as to borrow a sewing machine from my neighbor just to create part of the packaging I had designed.

When I made a mistake with the packaging, I briefly thought about letting it slide, but...no. I started all over and made sure that the end result matched my vision.

When I finally delivered the painting to my client, I wasn't sure what to expect. It was the first time I had opened myself up and hoped my art would make a difference in someone's life. After he had taken in the whole painting, he said, "This is like opening a Christmas present. It's a thousand times beyond my expectations."

He asked me how much it would be. But then he simply handed me the checkbook and said, "Write whatever you want."

I had never experienced anything like that before. I was in shock. It was a wonderful return on my investment on so many levels.

Customer focused

When I do paintings for my clients, I really make sure I do what is best for them. I even ask about their wall sizes and colors. I make every effort to understand them thoroughly. I never advise them to opt for a larger painting just so I can charge them more.

It takes some work to really get to know your regular clients, but with time, relationships often develop naturally. In the best-case scenarios, you and your clients will develop respect for each other. And from that can come customer loyalty and trust.

You are the most important part of your brand. How you carry yourself, your ethics and your values impact how your business is perceived. Make it something positive.

Chapter nine

IMPACT AND INFLUENCE PEOPLE EVERY TIME

Make your mark

One of the best things you can do to get ahead in business is know when to catch on to trends. A big trend right now that has a huge market is motivating and influencing people.

Many people are becoming "influencers," using social media to promote their unique brand to millions of followers. Hundreds of YouTube ads are coming and going with people trying to sell their ideas to others.

There is nothing more powerful than getting an emotional response from someone and making a lasting impact on them. Mark my word on this one, because I have seen the results of being able to influence others. I have made my customers cry out of joy! I will never forget the first client in business I had. I left an impact on him. My first painting I ever did as a commission was perhaps the most powerful experience. It was the first time I had opened up my self and let my art make a difference in people's lives.

I am always hearing stories of what my art has done to people who have bought it. I look beyond the check, and focus on creating a long-lasting impact on people. I strive to make sure they take away MUCH more than just the product or service offered to them. I make sure that when I am not handing out business cards to folks, they will be telling others about me still. When you touch people's hearts, they will go out of the way to do things for you! The more you understand them, the better!

It is also important to note, that you come before the product. You are the one that should influence the customer. Then, your product will carry yourself through and influence people on its own, as if it is a living form itself. At least with my art business, that is true. Art already has a large human touch attached to it. I could say that it naturally drives people's emotions and can make them happy. Despite art already having these connotations, I still always go to the next level on making sure my painting has surely influenced the customer.

If someone is accustomed to your highest quality of work, take it a step higher. Push to make their jaw drop. Even in the simplest of things, give that little bit extra. You want people telling everyone they know about you. Word-of-mouth advertising costs nothing and has big returns.

The benefits of exceeding expectations as a core value has an impact on many aspects of your life, from relationships to your own happiness. Be nice to your customers, make a difference in their life, and make your mark!

Chapter ten

WORK A $10-AN-HOUR JOB LIKE IT'S A $1000-AN-HOUR JOB

Work like you are earning 100 times more money

Always take what you are doing seriously. I've always thought that if someone is paying me, I HAVE to deliver results that are beyond what they wish for. The reason I keep repeating the point to really try more than just your best, is because repetition equals memorization. I want you to instill this value as your new standard. The title of this chapter, "Work a $10-an-hour job like it's a $1000 an hour job" is a formula bound to yield results.

Always think about this when you are about to do any sort of work. Especially when you have few customers at the start, you want to really go all in for each customer. Forget about how many hours you are working. If you have time, use all of it for what you are doing. Then, divide it up for each customer. It is like the supply and demand rule. If you have a low supply of customers at first, you want to give them more value through your services or products at first. It is similar to paying a higher price at for something when it is in low quantity.

Value each and everyone of your customers very much! If you have time, use every single minute of it to give them an abundance of service. This will naturally reflect how much you value them. You will see your returns later. By doing this, you will also be working for later benefits like free word-of-mouth advertising.

Now, let's go back to the topic of working a ten dollar an hour job like it's a thousand dollar an hour job. You may just get noticed in your job and get more opportunities if you used this formula. Whatever people pay you for doing work, multiply that by 100 and work it with that in mind. Almost every successful person I've read about and met has worked low paying jobs sometime in their life or even manual labor jobs.

Many people who have told me this, said that those jobs changed their mindset and were what prepared them for their careers. I remember one painting when a customer was offering to pay me a seemingly low amount. I tried to work with the customer. The initial amount they asked for was low, but the work I put into that customer was as if I was getting paid ten times the amount we discussed. The result of that did pay off. The customer actually paid me a pretty high price at the end! It was so casual, they just told me that they felt like bumping the check up a bit. The work I did for that customer made my genuine interest in doing my best really came out. So, forget about how many clients you have or how much you are getting paid in a job or business. Go all in, as if you are earning 100 times the money!

Specifically why being ordinary isn't okay

When you are starting a business, you simply cannot be mediocre. Mediocre is defined "as of moderate or low quality, value, ability, or performance, ordinary."

Your business has to grow, right? Ask yourself this, does ordinary grow? To grow at something you have to do more of it. Being static means you might as well not start any business at all. It is just one of the reasons small startups have a high failure rate. You must always grow.

Wake up earlier than your competition, innovate more than your competition, and work harder than your competition. Entrepreneur Grant Cardone said, "You sleep like you are rich. I'm up like I am broke."

Even once you attain a certain degree of success, you need to keep exceeding. Never forget that you aren't the only one competing in this world. On the other side of the globe, there will be a challenger awake and going to work.

Exceeding expectations will come naturally out of passion

I always give myself only two options. Either I will do something and I will be the best at it, or I will be mediocre and not do that thing. I want to give my best out there, because I know that mediocre is a definite formula for failure.

In my chapter about the Science of Rising Above People, I wrote about why you must be on top of your game to keep enjoying success. Whatever you do, be the best at it, or you will fall behind.

If you take interest in what you are doing, your passion will evolve naturally in you and your results. Think about the time you were doing something you liked. You probably didn't want anybody getting in your way while you were doing it, and two, you most likely wanted to keep going even when you ran out of time.

In business, don't let discouragement and other problems distract you and get in the way of what you are doing. If you're really motivated to keep working at something, you will work more than what is necessary. You'll be exceeding people's expectations without even knowing it.

Chapter eleven

SHOOT FOR THE MOON, BUT IF YOU MISS, DON'T BE HAPPY LANDING AMONG THE STARS

Don't compromise. Be satisfied only when you reach your goals.

Have you ever heard the saying "shoot for the moon, and even if you miss you will land among the stars"? It means that you should aim high. Even if you don't reach your goal, you will still land close to your goal. But I say shoot for the moon and land on the moon!

We live in a world where results are all that matters. Don't be satisfied when you "land among the stars." People like your parents, who love and care about you, might comfort you when you fail and say things like "at least you tried," or "at least you got this far."

They may feel better when saying this to you,

but are they helping you improve or just making you feel better about something you should not be feeling great about? Results matter! Aim high and achieve high.

It is nothing to get stressed out about, because you are working to achieve what you plan for. It's all on you and your will. If you truly want success, you will not be stressed to work the living daylights out of yourself to get to where you want to be. It is just a matter of setting small goals to get to the big goal. Lebron James said, "Every night on the court I give my all, and if I am not giving my 100 percent, I criticize myself."

Takeaway: GO UNTIL THE END.

Practice self-discipline and put in a little work every day. Bruce Lee once said that he "didn't fear the man who practiced a 1000 kicks in one day, but he feared the man who practiced one kick a day for a thousand days." Don't give yourself impossible tasks and then complain about not being able to go all the way. Think smart first, and then work hard to go to the end.

What I am saying is don't settle for less than you want. I have found myself very close to doing that. Sometimes I've had to work out of different mistakes just to meet the average! From there, it was my personal obligation to work double to get past the average! My instincts were that I had already worked more than I planned and that I should have settled.

At the end of the day though, I would still be

presenting average to my client. I worked until I got to where I wanted to be. You see, if you don't meet your expectations, anything below will just be average to you. You will still have untapped potential. Sure, you could have exceeded someone else's expectations, but you did not meet your own expectations. Through the years and my experiences so far, I have learned to stop settling. I have learned to realize when my potential is untapped and when it is at full use.

Chapter twelve

YOU CAN LEARN A LOT FROM
LUXURY BRANDS

An oft-cited quote attributed to various people, from Igor Stravinsky to Pablo Picasso, proposes that "Good artists copy, but great artists steal."

That quote, of course, can be construed in a negative way. However, think of it this way: Humans have been able to pass their knowledge onto successive generations. This is the reason we have dominated the planet and been able to go to the moon and back.

Accomplished people in all walks of life have learned from others before they became successful themselves. It doesn't matter whether you are self-taught or learned from an instructor.

The fact is, everyone has absorbed knowledge from someone else and then contributed it to the population and the next generation. Truly original ideas are rare. Even though we may not realize it, all ideas are modifications and improvements on previous ideas from other human beings just like us.

I have learned that next to working hard, one of the most beneficial things you can do for yourself is observe those around you who have accomplished what you want to accomplish. So why not take a lesson from the world's mega brands? They have a lot of valuable lessons to show and teach us about marketing, presentation, and business in general.

The allure of luxury

Although I can't buy a Rolls Royce just yet as a kid, I still enjoy walking into the dealership and seeing the cars up close. That makes some people say that I must like the "finest of things." But just because I enjoy looking at luxury cars doesn't mean I want to spend money. I don't have to buy one.

Maybe you aren't interested in things made by high-end manufacturers such as Rolls-Royce or Louis Vuitton, a $30 billion mega-brand that outperforms competitors such as Burberry and Gucci. However, it doesn't hurt to open yourself to these brands, as there is actually a lot we can learn from them about business.

Although it may be obvious that luxury products cost more because of materials and workmanship, there is additional markup for the brand-value such products offer.

There are some people who buy Louis Vuitton items who can't really afford to spend $600 on a pair of shoes or $1,000 on a handbag, but they do it anyway. People buy things to feel good, and Louis Vuitton has monetized this quirk of human nature.

I've looked at this through an entrepreneur's eye, and know it's a something that can help you raise your profit margin.

What Louis Vuitton and high-end brands can teach us about business

Merely saying the name "Louis Vuitton" sounds fancy, doesn't it? It brings to mind Paris, which leads to thoughts of fashion and art.

By associating itself with Paris and that city's reputation for style, Louis Vuitton has made its name one of the most powerful labels in the world of haute couture. It is on Forbes' list of the world's most valuable brands. And when a brand can imbue emotion into the things it makes, that company has learned a thing or two about how to run a business.

The ability to inject so much appeal into a couple of words is pretty amazing. The company took the "L" and put it over the "V" and created an identifiable and highly coveted monogram. The result is that the people feel good about owning a product featuring that trademark "LV."

So the first lesson we can take from Louis Vuitton and other high-end brands is to think about the first impression you make on potential customers and how can you make it impactful and positive.

The second lesson is to think about your commitment to yourself and your brand. Louis Vuitton has been committed to its one-of-a-kind monogram design for years. You know immediately that a bag or wallet is a Louis Vuitton when you see that monogram.

Change and innovation are good, but have to be handled carefully. You don't want to be all over the place. Let's take cars for example. Notice all the luxury and high-end cars out there like Bentley, Lamborghini, BMW, etc. Have you ever noticed how few design changes are made to these cars every year?

Compared to many other cars, these cars keep their grills and styling consistent. That is the reason you immediately recognize a Rolls-Royce or a Lamborghini. They only change small curves and edges each year. These subtle details make a difference, though, showing what is fresh and new.

Overall, staying committed to something in a brand is essential to building that brand. You want to work at creating recognition for your brand.

Brands that succeed are also ones that commit to their company's mission. For example, Rolls-Royce Motors has always followed an edict issued by company co-founder Henry Royce: "Strive for perfection in everything you do. Take the best that exists and make it better. If it doesn't exist, design it."

If you are ever lucky enough to take a seat inside a Rolls-Royce vehicle, just try to find a single piece of plastic. It may take you a while.

Many businesspeople say that perfection gets in the way of profitability, but perfection is something Rolls-Royce has continued to practice and still has had record-breaking sales in the last few years.

For me, perfection was getting the opportunity to ride in a Rolls-Royce Dawn with the top down!

Leave an impact

I call the impression your business makes, your "footprint." Keep in mind that once you've created that footprint, your brand is established. And that can be good or bad, depending how well you have worked at creating your business.

Although your footprint is permanent, it can be reshaped. You can fill it some or dig it a bit deeper. Companies with years of a good reputation, like Louis Vuitton, have a solid footprint, with customers confident about the company's commitment to quality.

Never get complacent about your footprint. There are countless brands out there that have built up their brand and then thought they could just coast. They stopped innovating and went downhill.

Your actions continually reshape your footprint. Amazon is an excellent example of this. The company is always pushing, and profiting more and more each day. Does that mean they have gotten complacent? Absolutely not! They keep closing more deals each year, and dominating their space. That is common to all successful mega-brands: They dominate their space and constantly push. They leave their footprint on every surface they land on in the marketplace.

The saying "the rich get richer" also applies to products: When all your friends have something that everybody says is good quality, you want to have it too, right? At that point, no one even has to explain or vouch for the product. When you are at this point, you know you have officially arrived. You have built your brand.

Ever since Louis Vuitton reached that point, they have been increasing their prices. They keep going up, exceeding Gucci, Burberry, Prada and other competitors.

Are their sales suffering? Nope, quite the contrary. Louis Vuitton is sending a message that says when you buy an LV product, it puts you in a class above Gucci. Louis Vuitton created a marketplace where every product they make is easier to sell than the one before.

The result: They dominate their industry.

Save room for the surprise

This is similar to the idea of "under promise and over deliver." Hold something back so that you have energy for a big finish. And this doesn't apply only to your business; it also works in social situations.

This approach can be used to influence people. It can be used to bring attention to you. It can change your reputation, maybe even surprise people. Let people get to know you and your products while still having something in reserve -- that "extra element" -- to blow them away afterward.

For example, in school if there is that one kid who doesn't ever do his homework, but then comes in with an A+ on a test, Isn't that going to surprise you and make you take notice of him?

Whereas, let's say there's a kid in class who impresses you on the first day by being studious and hard-working. Which kid are you more likely to talk about: The one who took you by surprise or the one who did exactly as you expected?

Luxury stores -- masters of the surprise

When it comes learning about how to save room for the surprise, luxury stores can serve as the perfect classroom. These stores set the stage beautifully, beginning with a large build-up of anticipation.

In a Louis Vuitton boutique, for instance, the bags are individually placed on shelves that are high out of reach. Limited-edition items are placed under glass. You can look but you can't touch.

But then the salesperson puts on white gloves

and brings the item within reach. After admiring that handbag from afar, now you can not only see it, but you also can feel it, and even smell that rich scent of leather.

It's similar with expensive jewelry and watches. Although it's common to put these items in glass case, the more special ones are sometimes tucked into in more elaborate and out-of-reach displays. The item teases from a distance. When it actually comes out of the glass and onto your hand, the excitement is palpable.

Compare that drama to seeing a watch or handbag displayed on a rack inside a Carson's or Macy's: There's no anticipation, no build-up, no surprise. No drama.

Kids can relate when it comes to toys. Getting a present for your birthday or Christmas meant unwrapping the gift, getting it out of a box or special packaging. Only then did you get to get a good look at it, touch it and yes! Play with it! The surprise is complete.

One of the ways I think differently after becoming an entrepreneur is when I walk into a car dealer, a department store, or a Louis Vuitton boutique, you name it! I tie it all to business. I see a different picture.

Keeping costs in mind

It's logical to assume that with such expensive products, Louis Vuitton is focused primarily on what it produces. But that's not completely true.

The company realizes perfection can get in the way of profitability.

Let's say there is a tailor down the street who sells suits for $10,000 each. That says a lot about the suits. But there's no reason to assume that suit business is a million-dollar company. Just because a business is in the luxury market, doesn't mean it makes a lot of profit. That tailor is most likely not rich if he or she is taking a lot of time to make those custom suits.

And consider an artist who might be selling paintings for $50,000 each. But if the artist turns out only two or three painting a year, he is making what many would consider a good living, but not necessarily achieving what one would consider truly wealthy.

This is why I admire Rolls-Royce. They have been able to sell a top-quality product while also making lots of money. As for Louis Vuitton, they aren't following the Rolls-Royce dictum of perfection. What they do is add value not just in quality materials, but also in the shopping experience.

A $25 Target bag might last just as long as a $2,000 one from Louis Vuitton; a $40 silk scarf you buy at Nordstrom Rack can hold up just as well as a $400 design you purchase at a Hermès boutique. But the high-end presentation, packaging, and great service can make all the difference.

Those high-end companies spend millions on designing luxurious and unique stores. They use exquisite materials for packaging. It all figures into getting customers to feel good about where they are spending their money.

Just watch what Rolex does

The story of Rolex is remarkable in that from its earliest days, the company has found a way to be creative in its marketing.

When Hans Wilsdorf and his brother-in-law Alfred David founded the company in 1905, they quickly took advantage of any opportunity to associate their watch with sporting events that they knew would capture the public's imagination.

Correctly assuming that swimmer Mercedes Gleitze would gain fame and media attention in 1927 for being the first British woman to cross the English Channel, the company made sure Gleitze swam with a fully waterproof Rolex Oyster Perpetual around her neck.

Rolex not only got attention, but they also could point to the fact that their watch had withstood whatever the English Channel could throw at it.

It was a promising start, but Wilsdorf and David always kept pushing further, never missing an opportunity to link their great watches to a competitive moment that everyone would watch.

The name Rolex became synonymous with celebrities, record-setting achievements, and innovations in technology. When Sir Malcolm Campbell set a land speed record in 1935 of more than 300 miles per hour, he wore a Rolex. Other adventurers and people who landed on the front pages of newspapers around the world always took the name Rolex along with them.

During the 20th century, Rolex watches went to the deepest parts of the ocean and to the top of Mt. Everest. Rolex had left its competitors in the dust and forged a reputation that endured even into the age of electronics and high-tech.

Rolex created a mechanical watch that was the gold standard of keeping time. The watches looked good on almost anyone, functioned in the face of the worst of what Mother Nature could throw their way, and kept "wowing!" the world.

Even to this day, Rolex still sponsors a wide range of sporting events -- whatever they can do that is true to their principles. It's no surprise that so many people know about Rolex and think of it as the best watch out there, even though there are many watches better than a Rolex.

More obscure names such as Jaeger-Lecoultre, Vacheron Constantin, Patek Phillipe, and IWC are all great watches. But only a true watch aficionado will know of these.

So I salute Rolex. They got themselves on the front pages of newspapers and landed on top of the watch world.

Chapter thirteen

THE SIMPLEST INVESTMENT THAT MOST PEOPLE SKIP ON

My experience with books and their value

I used to buy very few books. I admit that I would look at the price of a book and decide to take a pass. I used to not even hold much interest in reading to begin with!

These days, I buy books like I am buying food. I know that I'll get returns on books. Books are real investments. It is like when you put your money in a few different stocks, so out of these few stocks, one go up significantly and make you lots of money. It is the same with books. One book can change your life or shift your mindset, and a change in mindset equals a change in results.

Books can inspire you, change the way you think and lead you into new interests. People call anything investments these days, even a pair of

$600 shoes. Really? How much more of a return are those shoes going to give you than a pair of $100 shoes? People even go as far to say that things are an investment in happiness.

But things don't last. Knowledge lasts. I have read a few books I consider life changing. Because those books changed my life, I would have been willing to pay double or even triple the price. Also, books can be your mentors when the real ones aren't present!

Again, buying books is like buying stocks. The right book at the right time can make all the difference. When you find that book, read it over and over. Some of the books I have are unbelievably good investments. I have read them countless times when I have felt lost or wanted to get inspired. If you know where to seek knowledge, you'll likely to hit a jackpot full of it!

Choosing books that will actually teach you

I have quite a few friends who read voraciously every day. They will sit down with two inch-thick books at a time. I'm constantly getting books and read about half of them, but I guarantee I take away ten times more information than some of my friends.

I'm not against reading fiction, because you can still gain such skills as reading fast and proper grammar. But these days I'm looking for practical knowledge.

There are a few steps I take when picking out my books. I first read the table of contents, look at the names of the chapters, and then pick a chapter to read. These steps are pretty much enough to tell me if the book will be useful to me or not.

I like reading straight-to-the-point books on topics I'm interested in. I have come across some books that I knew were right for me at first sight. Keep digging until you find these types of books.

Sometimes books become unnecessarily long because of page-consuming stories. Stories and examples explaining the concepts that books provide are beneficial to a certain extent. You need to decide when to stop reading the examples. If you understand the concept and have practically memorized it, there is no point in reading the examples.

I have a history of getting annoyed with some books because the authors just keep rambling and then the book gets boring. The author can write however much he or she wants, but you get to decide when it comes to what you want to learn from the book. I have used this strategy, and I have seen a noticeable difference in not only the knowledge I retain, but also how I apply what I have learned.

Some people say they prefer fiction over non-fiction. Well, the sad truth is that reading only fiction might make you better at English, but it won't teach you practical knowledge. There are certain types of genres that can be beneficial, including historical fiction, realistic fiction, and sci-fi. These genres often are based on real life subjects like history and science.

They will impart knowledge about the human condition, but the knowledge might not be useful right away.

My parents wanted my reading habits to be more like my friend who loved the Harry Potter series. I never used to be a good reader and never could be like that kid. I didn't care about Harry Potter and I still don't. I get more value and enjoyment from reading several shorter non-fiction books a week than a single two-inch thick fantasy novel.

What if you don't like to read?

These days, sitting in a comfy chair with a hardcover book isn't the only way to "read." Audiobooks and ebooks are one solution. And you can listen while you do other things, like walk or get chores done.

Sometimes, people who say they don't like to read haven't really found books that interest them.

Being an entrepreneur has changed the way I think about reading, which I never used to do for more than a day before losing interest.

At school, I used to get reading logs to fill out what I read and then had to get my parents to sign off on them. Those logs made me panic. Sometimes I would have to quickly read the few days before the log was due. All those years I had been forced to read and never wanted to do it.

But since I entered high school, I started finding topics that interest me, and therefore increased my reading. Now, I have tripled my reading. I never really read entire books, one after another. Instead, I pick books that appeal to me and read whatever sections and chapters interest me. Sometimes I return to old books, and read parts again. This is what makes me retain knowledge and ensure I take something away from the book.

So, don't give up on books even if you say you don't like to read. Try dipping into several books on topics that interest you. Pick a genre you like and only read what appeals to you. When you like something, you will not think of reading as work. You will eventually develop a liking for reading. After all, repetition creates a habit.

Once you have a solid habit of reading, then try reading other subjects or genres. Don't worry about not being a good reader. I never used to read very fast. That worry distracted me from actually focusing on what I was reading.

Just ignore those concerns about "not being a good reader," or "not being a fast reader." Focus instead on the book that's in front of you.

Don't read because you will be admired for being a voracious reader, and don't read to make your parents happy. Rather, read to win in life. Read to gain knowledge that you can apply to your life and see the results.

Chapter fourteen

HOW TO COME UP WITH BUSINESS IDEAS

Getting the idea

I like to think of problems as opportunities. Whenever you encounter a problem, brainstorm a few ways to fix it. You'll be surprised at how many problems you simply dismiss or ignore.

Think about all the times you are unhappy. Look for patterns of what causes unhappiness. Maybe it is an inconvenience. Think about what would make your life easier. Kids sometimes talk about superpowers that would make their life great. What would make your life great?

Some of your ideas may seem crazy, but don't just dismiss them. New ideas often seem crazy, or at least "different." What some people call crazy, others might label "brilliant." Remember: There was a time when everyone thought the world was flat and that the sun revolved around the earth. Crazy, right?

I recommend keeping a record of all your thoughts and ideas. You might be amazed at how much you have thought of throughout the day. Write every idea down! Then, you can go back later and see if they still seem like good ideas to you.

Even with this book, I used to come downstairs from my bedroom to my study room at midnight to capture an idea that I didn't want to forget. If I hadn't done that, I would have lost pages of good material for this book.

If one of your ideas keeps speaking to you, listen to it. It might just be business gold!

Once ideas are gone, they are gone

Nothing is more disheartening or frustrating than seeing another person succeed using the same idea you had. You need to take action when your brainstorm hits. Don't let ideas sit around for ages, but at the same time don't waste energy fretting about someone trying to steal your ideas.

I believe that a truly original idea will always be unique to that person. Every idea counts, because you never know when a certain idea might be gold.

Many people just say "I'll do this tomorrow," or "I'll write my idea down later." Stop dismissing so many ideas by making excuses! Be compulsive about it if you have to. I'm pretty compulsive about it.

Once you start getting in the "work-hard vibe," or the entrepreneur lifestyle of waking up early and working hard, you might always be thinking. Sometimes, if I work late then go to bed, I keep thinking about what I was doing. Don't try to turn your brain off. Just make sure you capture any ideas or thoughts you have.

Creativity doesn't have an on/off switch

Never force yourself to come up with ideas. When someone puts a time limit on you and says come up with ideas, those ideas are likely to be pretty lame.

The best ideas come from seeing a problem in the world -- or just in your life -- and coming up with a solution. Ideas need to be grounded in reality. It is ridiculous to say that you want to start a business, make money, and need an idea by next week. That sounds like you simply want to make money, so you need an idea, any idea will do. You have no interest in benefiting mankind.

If you don't know why you are doing something and what purpose you have in life, the ideas will not come. Even if you do come up with ideas, those ideas will lack passion and are likely doomed to fail.

There are a few business clubs at my school, none of which I joined the first year of high school, even when I knew I liked business. Why didn't I join? One reason: They involved competing for a business idea among hundreds of other kids with a similar level of intelligence. It didn't seem like it was worth my time, when I knew that if I want to grow a business on my own, I could do my own research, find an investor, and make it happen. The competition felt more like a distraction. I am not naive in any way, as I do recognize the value that being in these clubs offer. However, this is just my scenario here.

If you're willing to do the hard work of research, you don't need someone to help you. I tried asking my dad for some pointers. He has an MBA from an Ivy League school, but never started any sort of business. When I asked him how to start a business, he said I was too young and that I should just focus on school and wait to learn about business in college. I'm glad I ignored that advice!

If I had to put credit somewhere, it would be with YouTube and the informative videos I found there. Most people know me for my business and art, but those who know me well also know that I am an engineering nerd. I know pretty much how all engines work, and I can name most parts of an airplane and car. And it's all thanks to YouTube.

You don't need to wait for people to come and teach you things. You don't need someone to hand you a certificate and say you are a business person. Sure, getting an MBA helps a lot, but starting from scratch and and doing your own research will teach you so much.

The definition of an entrepreneur is a person who starts a business and is willing to take risks in order to make money. When you start with even less knowledge compared to someone with an MBA, you learn not only about the business itself, but also about things like life-values and a solid work ethic.

It all came together for me and inspired me to write this book. I wanted to share with others who might be thinking about starting a business, the fact that entrepreneurship can change the way you think and see everything. I know it did that for me!

The concept -- not the product -- makes the business

The most common excuse I hear from people about why they aren't starting a business is not being able to come up with a good idea.

Here's a tip: Don't think your idea has to be super brilliant.

Sure your business should be unique, but it doesn't have to be as unique as you might think. To get the cash flow started, you'll need more than just a product. You'll need a concept too. A concept ensures that your business is an open-ended process. That means you have a business that you can run every day, not simply a project that makes you money but has an end date.

For example, the company Scrub Daddy© used the concept of their special plastic, which hardens or softens depending on the water temperature it's exposed to. With consumer products, it's very important to be scalable. Otherwise, you just sell your product out and then you're done. A single product cannot make a business.

Concepts can be as general as a consulting firm or landscaping business, for instance. These are very broad niches you can occupy. If you want to start making money and get to work, find niches like this and just start working.

For me, art is a concept, not one product. I generate so many types of art that it's not just individual projects; it's a business. I didn't come up with a brilliant idea. I created an ongoing business from the concept of creating art and providing people with the best service.

So instead of brainstorming one idea, just start doing something in an area where you can help people. A consulting business is a good example of this.

You can help people, or consult, in any way you chose. I am writing this book while being a kid-entrepreneur to help people discover new trains of thought and spark interest in the fascinating subject of entrepreneurship.

Writing a book is a way of helping people. Starting a YouTube channel where you post informative or entertaining videos is another way to help people and start a business at the same time.

Whatever concept and niche you are thinking about, work to be the best. If you are struggling for ideas, just pick a niche such as consulting, teaching, landscaping, contracting -- whatever interests you and where you believe you can do your best work.

Chapter fifteen

MISTAKES ARE INVESTMENTS

Your biggest mistake can bring you your biggest advantage

Stop thinking so much about what you did wrong. So many people get discouraged because society often focuses on mistakes and things that go awry.

I think people should encourage others to think about what's possible, rather than reminding them about their mistakes.

Whenever you make a mistake, turn it into a lesson. When you fail at something, figure out what went wrong. And there's your payoff from a mistake: You get smarter. So instead of feeling bad about what happened, you have something to feel good about.

As for the really big mistakes, they're just even bigger lessons, right?

A lesson learned pays for that expensive mistake

Let's say you just lost a bunch of money after you really messed up. What if I told you that that loss was worth every penny?

For example: Ferraris are expensive, not just to buy but also to maintain. Just one punctured tire can cost $500 to repair. And that's just a tire puncture. What about a repair that can run $2,000 to $3,000?

In this scenario, you take your Ferrari (lucky you!) to a skilled mechanic for repairs. The repairs are, indeed, expensive, but then you learn that's only partly because you own a Ferrari. You took an ever bigger hit because you were charged double what a different, equally skilled Ferrari mechanic would have charged.

It may sound crazy but I think you should look at it this way: You'll never forget the time you messed up and didn't do your research. You paid too much to get your Ferrari fixed. It was an expensive lesson, of course, but it's one you certainly won't forget. (As for that first mechanic, he can forget about ever seeing you again.)

Similarly, the harder you have to work for something the more you value it. Spend your hard-earned cash on the latest cell phone and you'll know where it is every minute of the day. But if someone simply gave you a new phone, how careful would you be with it?

One time I needed to replace the battery of my watch. I had opened the back of a watch before, but that one was less complicated. This one had a pressure-fitted back. I managed to open it properly, but then I ran into trouble when I tried to put the back on again. I struggled to make it fit. I thought I was being careful, but I don't think I used the right tools.

I finally took the watch to a repair shop, where they told me that I had damaged an O-ring that went on the cover. At this point, I got kind of nervous. Thankfully, they said the same O-ring would work this time, and that it wasn't in too bad of a shape. However, I would have to buy a new one the next time the battery needed to be changed. It was pretty expensive. On top of that, I had to pay for the repair. So now I really think twice before attempting to do any sort of maintenance on my watches myself. I would say that the mistake was well worth the money I lost though, because it was an appropriate loss for the weight of the lesson I learned.

I also made a mistake the first time I priced my paintings for sale in a gallery. I was naive and priced them too high. I was conflicted about parting with my paintings, so I thought that even if people didn't buy any of them, I would be ok with that. Conversely, if a painting did sell, all that money would make me feel better!

But I was embarrassed when I realized that my prices were higher than any of the established artists also on display in the gallery. Yes, my art could have been worth the price I put on the paintings, but the reality was that I was an unknown to everyone. I had not established my brand. My mistake was pretty big so the lesson really hit home. I turned my mistake into an investment in knowledge.

If you make a mistake with something you don't value much, it's no big deal. But if a mistake keeps preying on your mind, that probably means you value the lesson more than the cost of the mistake!

Your effort is never really wasted

Like mistakes, failure has its benefits too. American inventor Charles Kettering said, "Ninety-nine percent of success is built on failure."

Even if you do not earn a single dollar at the end of three years of working day and night, don't think you worked for nothing. You became a stronger machine. When you commit to rise above every failure you face, eventually you will rise so high that nobody can take you down.

There is a reason many rich people grew up poor. Whether you win or fail, you are always learning. Knowledge is valuable; it makes you a stronger and more capable machine for the next endeavor.

Don't look down on those who fail

Don't discount all the people who have tried and failed. People who are at the bottom who have tried and failed could be just as smart as those who have succeeded. In fact, they could be even wiser, because what they have been through has made them stronger and more prepared for the next challenge. Keep your ears open to everyone. A lot of people won't be perfect, but they will have those few things you can learn from.

Steve Jobs could have been similarly smart when he was fired from Pixar as when he scored big with Apple. It is just about how the world perceived him when he finally won at business. He was not fired for his lack of intelligence. People just considered him much more intelligent when he actually did achieve success. Society often sees the end results of people, and doesn't pay attention to how they got there.

I know what it feels like when you have to struggle and worry about failing. I have worried about hoped-for dreams not coming true. You can work hard and apply all the knowledge you've gained, and yet still fail.

If you keep pushing, you always have to accept the risk of failure. My point is that when someone is going through tough times, has worked really hard but has also failed repeatedly, don't necessarily judge them to be dumb. They have just gone down a slightly different path and perhaps made just a couple of decisions that threw them off track. Besides, they will probably learn a couple life lessons from their failures that you would have yet to learn!

Chapter sixteen

LISTENING TO THE RIGHT PEOPLE

Keep your ears and your mind open

Finding good advice is a bit like mining for gold. You come across a lot of rock and debris, but the mix also includes little chunks of something precious and valuable.

Don't limit your sources; take in a broad range of advice, even if at first you don't think someone is qualified to advise you. Don't make assumptions about what they might or might not know. Think about what you're being told and sort out what is valuable. Tuning out someone just because they aren't in business could be a lost opportunity: You might miss out on a big pot of gold!

Knowing who to listen to

With a world full of noise and distraction, it can be hard to focus and find the right people to take trusted advice from. There are so many contradicting opinions.

When you're looking for mentors, teachers, or inspiring figures to be your role models, it can be hard to sort out who to trust. This is especially true in business. Because backgrounds differ, two equally successful entrepreneurs could both offer opposite pieces of advice.

Even if both are successful, they each can have advice that is unique to their own situation and background in business. Every entrepreneur takes their own path, and specializes in something. They all have faced different events, successes, and failures. The sum of these experiences affects the kind of advice they will give. One tip might work well for one person, but not for another.

The key is to find people who are like you, or like what you would like to be in several years. Narrow the field down to these few people and just listen to them.

But, this isn't always easy. I have heard people such as American businessman and investor Mark Cuban say, "don't follow your passion." On the other hand, Belarusian-American author and entrepreneur Gary Vaynerchuk's book specifically tells people to have passion in the very first chapter.

Contradictory? Maybe -- but these two things can be more nuanced than it would appear. "Shark Tank's" Daymond John followed his passion of clothing, which turned into the mega-brand FUBU. But some successful people say entrepreneurs should simply focus on getting good at something they may or may not like.

There's also the issue of people who haven't yet identified their passion. Or their passion isn't formed enough to be monetized.

But what about those who already have a passion and know that passion can be monetized and scaled up? Daymond John did this with FUBU, while always being passionate about fashion. I myself, monetized my passion. I was not a kid who did not know what my passion was. I knew what my passion was for a long time and knew I could make money on it if I worked really hard at it. Long story short, different people's advice can apply to different people's situations.

Chapter seventeen

FACING NEGATIVE CRITICISM HEAD-ON

How to identify negative criticism

Criticism comes in two forms: constructive and negative. It can be hard to find people who are qualified to offer constructive criticism. As for the negative critics, the more you achieve, the more populous they can become.

People who offer only negative criticism aren't looking to help you improve. Most of the time they criticize you because they are jealous or have something against you. These critics often have no idea what they are talking about.

The good news is that when you start getting haters like this, it means you are becoming successful and gaining attention. Embrace it, don't fight it. Don't try to get revenge with your actions; get revenge with your success. Focus on those who support you and appreciate your work.

Even if you are not succeeding yet and you are

being put down, try to block negative people from your thoughts and work. Don't tune out constructive criticism though. That is what helps you improve!

How to cope with it

My tip for coping with negative criticism is fill your mind with positive thoughts. Get busy with your work and stay away from negative people and places.

If you are struggling with negative criticism, avoid those people and become so busy that you don't have time for the self-doubt those people are trying to unload on you.

Think of yourself as a robot. You don't have the ability to feel sad or hurt from negativity. You just have the ability to work! Don't let these distractions slow your progress. Keep looking forward and stay focused.

When you get busy with your own work, you will be less affected by outside distractions. This is the No. 1 thing that has worked for me and even raised my happiness levels. It can also cool your temper.

The main thing to remember is that when you flood your mind with something else, there's no room for negative thoughts.

My experiences

The reason I know about negative criticism and bullying is because I've been through it.

I really started using these coping skills in high school, when one of my friends turned his back on me. Then, my other friends did the same.

There were some problems in elementary school, but they came back in high school after I introduced a couple of my friends to each other. One friend, I'll call him "Dan" (not his real name), didn't have anyone else to hang out with, so I made sure I sat with him at lunch. Before too long, Dan and the other friend I had introduced him to had expanded their network of friends. Then the bigger group, led by Dan, pushed me out: literally and figuratively.

They called me racist names and swore at me. After I went to the student dean about the issue, Dan made fun of me for seeking help. The bullying felt relentless.

The group teased me about my art, about my clothes, about being a "nerd." In the meantime, I was getting such positive feedback from people across the country about my paintings.

So I decided to fill my head with business and not leave room for negativity. That is when I realized that the best revenge on Dan would be to become super-successful.

The best way to do this was to not even think of him, not think of the competition, and just work.

And look at me now: I am turning that same

experience into money by writing about it! I turned the anger into my own success.

Finding motivation

Today, there are countless places to look for motivation. People now have websites dedicated solely to motivation.

It's a popular niche, and not just for entrepreneurs. These days it seems like everyone wants to motivate everyone else.

Whether it be exercising, eating healthier, or handling stress, everyone needs motivation to do the things they don't like to do or that are hard for them.

If you want to self-motivate, you can read books about inspiring people, watch videos or just search for information on the internet. Maybe this book has motivated you or inspired you in some way!!

I like to find motivation via YouTube. In my opinion, it's the single best place for endless amounts of free motivation. Just type "motivation" in the search bar and off you go.

The main goal here is to change your negative way of thinking and start a new train of thought. You know how when you watch a movie you feel refreshed, relaxed, or maybe even changed after watching it? The vibe of the movie stays with you. Just like that, finding new people or things that motivate you will recharge and refocus your mindset.

Watching the same motivational videos all the

time can become useless after a while. So find new people to motivate you. Even the ones who might put you off have something to offer and are worth listening to. Just be sure to focus on the skills and not the person!

Conversely, if you find someone you really like, stick with that person. Don't have too many people you follow for inspiration. The result will be contradictory messages that will distract you from the path you want to be on.

Find someone who is like the person you want to become, then use them as a mentor by listening to and then learning from them. The best kind of motivation mentors and inspirational people are the ones that you can learn a lot from and be impacted by through their books and videos without even ever meeting them.

Chapter eighteen

HAPPINESS PHENOMENON

The phenomenon and how I experienced it

At one point during summer break, I suddenly realized that I was unusually happy being a hard-working entrepreneur.

While some kids might goof off in summer and adults might keep telling them to relax and take a break, I ignored that advice and felt extremely productive and happy. I was doing something that challenged me, but it was also something I liked.

Then I decided to do something that I had been thinking about for a while. I would live like all the successful people I had read about and had been motivated by. And by that I don't meant having a life filled with cars, a big house and fancy watches. Those things don't matter; they are the motivators and rewards that come afterward.

I would wake up early, try to beat the sun up, exercise right in the morning, and then have my schedule of things to do completely full.

It was odd that I felt no stress despite facing a daily to-do list that filled two pages with bullet points. Now I realize why: If I were in school and had a schedule like this, I would be completely stressed out because the list represented things that someone told me I had to do. Teachers, parents, the fear of low grades, all would factor into my stress.

In contrast, my summer schedule was self-imposed. I could just have easily taken it easy and ended the summer by going to camps and relaxing. I had decided to do this because I had drive, and it was something I wanted to do for myself. In school, I am forced to go in and out of classes all day, all while not particularly interested in doing some of the things I have to do there.

A not so purposeful class, in my opinion, that I took in school was a mandatory Honors Biology class. The first day I came in, I knew it wasn't right for me. The last day of that class, I felt I had wasted time taking the class. But, I gave myself some time to wait and see if that class did something for me. But no. I still think it shouldn't be listed as a required class. If you know that you are not going to be a doctor, what is the point of learning so much and then just forgetting about it? A certain amount of the knowledge was not wasted, but the depth of biology that class brought me into seemed pointless.

I would understand if the class had been some kind of mandatory business course. I say this not because this is what I like, but no matter what you do in life, you will have to know about money and investing.

I remember coming in at the first day of school. The teacher said that this class was going to teach you work ethic like no other. He specifically told the class, "many of you might not even want to be doctors, but you will learn tremendous skills and work ethic." So, this was the main purpose of the class. After thinking about it, I realized the problem with this. The two things you need in order to succeed in a situation like this are either drive or passion. You can have both, or you can have one or the other. The problem for me was, I didn't have either of those, so it was difficult to succeed in that class without having stress and working without any motivation.

I still maintained my GPA but the cost was a lot of unnecessary stress and sleep deprivation. Maybe you could say I had a little bit drive, if only to show colleges that I could make it through an honors science class as a freshman. But the class didn't motivate me. I just felt like I had a big weight over me that would drop if I didn't keep holding it up. It felt like I was stuck in a prison. I felt as though I was the slave of all the teachers and everyone that wanted me to do well in that class. There is a difference between that and getting up at 6:00 to work out of my own will during my summer break.

Passion comes out of interest and joy from working hard at something. Drive can be the reason for doing something you don't like and then becoming great at it. If you take a job you don't like, but are doing it because you want to really learn something and help yourself and your family, I believe that is drive.

Happiness can come when you are working hard while being fueled by either of these things. Drive can involve doing something you don't like, but at the same time you can still be happy doing it because you are motivated. You can even be motivated to motivate yourself and persevere!

Work ethic tied to happiness

We are born to work. That's not a negative thing. There is a reason our souls are morphed into a physical form with hands and feet. We humans, are made to work!

Don't let that scare you because being active is what will bring you happiness. I'll prove we are meant to work right now. If you were stuck inside a room for 48 hours, what would happen? You would probably become a maniac within just a couple of hours.

You would get depressed and maybe freak out about your situation. We simply cannot just sit and do nothing. We are not born for that. So, why do people complain about working hard? It is because we are so focused on the notion that we have to get to Friday. After Friday is over, we finally have the weekend. And then what? Oh no! It's Monday.

Everybody acts like they have to get past Monday, like it shouldn't even exist. This doesn't make sense. Think about how this affects your happiness levels, and how many people around you reinforce this thought.

Every day should have the same feel of "Thank god it's Friday." Don't goof off when Friday comes, and don't get bogged down when Monday rolls around. Again, it all comes down to changing your mindset about this, and that starts with a change in your actions.

Why we think relaxation is tied to happiness

As winter break approaches, so many kids can be overheard talking about "just chilling over break." It is as if the definition of relaxation is just doing nothing. That is ridiculous.

Some adults and kids take it easy when they take a break from work, which is okay. You do need short breaks for your mind and body to physically keep working. The respite from doing work you don't enjoy can bring temporary happiness. But it's just a short step from avoiding work and lingering your way into laziness, and that's where you have to be careful.

Many people are doing work without any drive or passion. Escaping that work is what they think will yield happiness. For example, if you are working at a job you don't like, but have a goal to climb the corporate ladder, that's what drives your work ethic.

I used to really dislike geometry. But I worked hard in class because I knew I would use math in business, and genuinely wanted to be good with numbers. Maybe I didn't like math, but I was driven to do better at it, and guess what? I got to a point where I was getting consistent A's. I was so happy about this, I didn't even consider relaxation a reason to be happy. I noticed I was actually happier to be working on math.

During spring break, I continued working on a small online venture. I was working pretty hard because everything was new to me, but I was happier and I felt that I had gotten much more done than the last spring break.

At first, it was hard for me to realize what was I was feeling. I frankly felt good about not "just chilling" during spring break. In just one week, I had come up with the plan, created a real product and made some sales.

I really felt like this break from school was fulfilling. When everybody else dreaded returning to school, I was more than satisfied and ready to go!

A short, but intriguing thought on happiness

Being a young entrepreneur and doing business everyday while working really hard, I've noticed something interesting about happiness. When I am looking forward to doing something, happiness is really high. But when I actually get to the moment, my happiness starts to wane. I think that's because you've achieved your dream. Allow me to explain.

Why are we always dreaming? Why are kids always looking for new toys? Why do we watch YouTube videos or TV about the products we love?

It is all because dreaming about the next thing we desire is what brings that moment of happiness. It is why we always want new things after we get what we want. When we have things we want, there is less excitement to it. It is in front of our eyes, we can see it, feel it, and it is always there. The appeal dims.

This also applies to experiences. Once you are on the roller coaster, you are excited. However, think about how excited you are at the moment before getting on the roller coaster. Think about how thrilled you are even before you sit on the roller coaster, anticipating it. Before you even get to the amusement park, you are looking forward to the ride. All those hours of waiting make you happy because of the thought of that ride ahead of you. Sometimes the anticipation can be even more thrilling than the ride itself.

I don't think it is bad to keep wanting the next thing, as long as you work for it. Should you be content with what you have? Absolutely. Should you stop asking for more? Not necessarily.

If that pushes you to work even harder, it's a plus. Be happy with what you have, but also keep dreaming. Not being happy with what you have will make you miserable. I say: Be thankful for the present, and ambitious for the future.

Chapter nineteen

ENTREPRENEURSHIP BROUGHT ME A NEW LIFESTYLE

Applying the values of entrepreneurship produce a lifestyle, not just a business

The purpose of my writing this book was to share the values that I learned and put into action as an entrepreneur. This book is not my life story. I have learned a lot, and still have much more to learn through my journey. However, I have definitely come to realize how the values of being an entrepreneur lead to a certain lifestyle.

It is a lifestyle full of hard work, confidence, gained social-skills, learning, full commitment, lots of perseverance, maximum effort, and accomplishment. Entrepreneurship produces an improved work ethic, better relationships, and an ability to get along with others.

I have seen much growth in myself that has by

far surprised me and surpassed my expectations. I am growing and learning every day.

Of course, when I say "lifestyle," I don't mean a life with more materialistic things. Success doesn't mean making a lot of money. Success means being content with your life, whether you have a lot or you don't.

The application of entrepreneurship produces both materialistic gains and increased happiness.

Conclusion

Every day when you wake up, be positive and look forward to making the most of each day. Don't take any day for granted. We are blessed with every day that is given to us.

Don't waste this time. Make the most of it, not just by working, but also living each day with happiness. We need more people to put work and happiness together. They should not be in two different worlds.

People should look forward to producing something new each day. Entrepreneurship as a kid has opened a new path for me and provided me with so many opportunities and ideas. Most of all though, it has taught me valuable lessons about life.

Being an entrepreneur is not just about creating a business and making money. It is about so much more. To me, being an entrepreneur doesn't simply mean starting businesses. I believe that everyone has an inner entrepreneur that they can bring out. I think being an entrepreneur simply means using all the values I mentioned in this book. You can be like an entrepreneur by innovating, working hard wherever you are, being creative, and by coming up with ideas to persevere through any sort of obstacle life throws at you.

The values of entrepreneurship are things that can be applied if you are in school, at a job, or like me! I am blown away with all the change and new opportunities that have arisen from creating a business as a kid. I not only monetized my passion, but I also started thinking differently.

I have applied everything I talked about in this book to my life. I expanded the business aspect to a broader life aspect. I have connected everything I learned to a much larger picture. Again, It doesn't matter if you are a businessperson or not. What I want you to do, now that you've read the book, is to apply the information I've given you to your life.

The insight I offer to you is only as powerful as you make it. I want you to shape a change in your mindset, just as I did. If you have any questions, please feel free to send me an email at sunnydeshpande777@gmail.com and I'll be happy to help you.

NOTES

NOTES

NOTES

NOTES